Beatitudes and Beads

Rosary Meditations on Blessedness

Philip Neri Powell, OP

One Liguori Drive
Liguori MO 63057-9999

Imprimi Potest: Thomas D. Picton, C.Ss.R.
Provincial, Denver Province, The Redemptorists

Published by Liguori Publications, Liguori, Missouri 63057, USA
To order, call 800-325-9521, www.liguori.org.

© 2010 Philip Neri Powell, OP

ISBN 978-0-7648-1966-7

All rights reserved. No part of this publication may be reproduced, stored in a retrieval system, or transmitted in any form or by any means—electronic, mechanical, photocopy, recording, or any other—except for brief quotations in printed reviews, without the prior written permission of Liguori Publications.

The material in this pamphlet is adapted from a chapter in *Treasures Holy and Mystical: A Devotional Journey for Today's Catholics* (Liguori Publications 2010), © 2010 Philip Neri Powell, OP.

Scripture texts in this work are taken from the *New American Bible with Revised New Testament and Revised Psalms* © 1991, 1986, 1970 Confraternity of Christian Doctrine, Washington, D.C. and are used by permission of the copyright owner. All Rights Reserved. No part of the *New American Bible* may be reproduced in any form without permission in writing from the copyright owner.

Liguori Publications, a nonprofit corporation, is an apostolate of the Redemptorists (redemptorists.com).

Printed in the United States of America
14 13 12 11 10   5 4 3 2 1

Introduction

Praying this rosary and meditating on the mysteries of blessedness will bring you closer to the heart of Christ's teaching found in his Sermon on the Mount (Matthew 5—7). Jesus teaches that we find his happiness through humility, repentance, and charity.

When we are persecuted for preaching his Word, we are to rely solely on the grace of his Holy Spirit to give us the words for making peace. When we confront our own pride, obstinacy, and apathy, we are bound in obedience to repent and seek reconciliation. Our happiness in Christ is not assured because we're right or powerful or feared. We inherit the kingdom when we face insult, persecution, and lies with gladness, charity, and mercy.

The following prayer is designed for a ten-decade rosary. To pray it with a five-decade rosary, use each set of ten beads twice or pray five decades on alternating days.

Crucifix: *Sign of the Cross (+)*

Beatitude Promise (TOGETHER)

Poor in spirit, we weep for our sins and rejoice in Christ's comfort; we hunger and thirst for his righteousness and submit ourselves to his teaching. Longing to be merciful and pure of heart, we strive to be peacemakers for his sake even in the midst of persecution. Amen.

Leader: Lord Jesus, gathering your faithful disciples around you, you taught them the Way of Blessedness, our path to happiness here on earth and in the life to come. Hear us as we follow your Way in prayer and bless us with all the gifts we need to enjoy the beauty made manifest in your Blessed Mother. Lead us to your Sacred Heart, where our eyes will see and our ears will hear. Amen.

(Bead 1, together) Our Father…

(Beads 2, 3, and 4, together) Mother Mary, Blessed of God, bearer of the Word made flesh, from your virgin womb came Christ Jesus, the Lord, our way to heavenly peace. Be with us now and when we stray. Amen.

(Bead 5, leader) Happy are those who follow the path of humility and hope. Happy are those who carry the cross of Christ for his sake. Happy are we who pray for his gift of peace.

FIRST DECADE
Blessedness

Leader: From his abundant goodness, the Lord provides all we need for our happiness.

Meditation

The perfectly lived Christian life is a life of happiness and peace. We might think this means that no Christian will ever suffer from sadness or bouts of turmoil. Not so. The happiness Christ promises to his followers is not a placid serenity or the unmovable calm of a Zen Buddhist monk sitting in meditation.

Rather, Christian happiness is the peace we feel when we know the path we follow leads to the perfection of our purpose as lovers of God. Happiness now depends entirely on our trust in the happiness to come in heaven.

Practically speaking, this means that any sadness we feel, any turmoil we experience, pales beside the grand drama of our eternal lives in God in heaven. Christ and his Church are the rock from which we venture out into the world. Securely anchored to the faith of the Body, we can be at perfect peace knowing that nothing on this earth can come between God and his people. The Sermon on the Mount teaches us exactly what this peace entails and how we not only maintain our hold on God but strengthen that hold as well.

Each beatitude gives us an attitude to adopt and a course of action to take. Faithfully followed, they will bring us closer and closer to the ideal of the perfect Christian life. Thanks be to God that we do not tread the Way of Christ alone! God's treasury of grace is inexhaustible, boundless, and given to us without condition. Though freely given, we must receive these graces to put them to work.

To receive God's gifts, we have only to dispose our hearts and minds to believe and practice the virtues contained in the beatitudes. The exercise of graced virtue builds spiritual muscle and makes the journey to Christ's perfection less strenuous on the soul and more likely to succeed. However, if the journey is taken alone—without family, friends, neighbors, the Church—the stress of carrying the cross will end in defeat.

In all the beatitudes, Jesus clearly indicates that it is the Church being Christ together that is blessed with the kingdom and the earth as their inheritance.

*(**Ten beads, together**)* Mother Mary… *(page 4)*

Beatitude Promise (TOGETHER) *(page 4)*

SECOND DECADE
Blessedness of a poor spirit

Leader: "Blessed are the poor in spirit, for theirs is the kingdom of heaven."

Meditation

A common feature of murder-mystery novels is the presumptuous heir, the child or wife or brother who presumes he or she is the heir to the murdered millionaire's fortune. Suspicious minds begin to calculate the ways in which the puffed-up fortune-seeker might have helped their benefactor into the afterlife before his time. The detective-hero often pesters the heir until a better suspect comes along.

In the meantime, most everyone seems content to assume that the one with the most to gain by the death of the millionaire is the one who killed him. With this assumption goes all the gossip, taunts, and derision those left out of the will can muster.

The presumptive heir would be better served by being poor in spirit and assuming nothing about the inheritance. Jesus teaches those gathered that the kingdom of God falls to those who live in worship and awe of the Father, not in prideful spite or the audacious pursuit of worldly kingdoms.

The poor spirit is not bereft of fire or lacking in zeal. Jesus isn't telling us to take on the spirit of a whipped stray found in a dumpster. The spiritual poverty we seek is the humility found in the one who knows that his very life is totally dependent on the love of God.

A humble Christian remembers she is made from the dirt of the earth and given life by the breath of the Creator. Without the loving will of God to bring us up from the ash, we would not be. And absent God's love for us after our creation, we would cease to be.

Knowing this truth, living in the knowledge of our origins and what we would be without divine love, we should nourish a rich sense of humility and uproot any opposing audacity that threatens to choke out God's light. Yes, we are heirs to the kingdom if we are poor in spirit. But this isn't a cause for prideful boasting. Quite the opposite—

as humble heirs to the fortunes of merit amassed through the cross, we are grateful and rejoice in our good favor.

(Ten beads, together) Mother Mary… *(page 4)*

Beatitude Promise (TOGETHER) *(page 4)*

~~~~~~~~~~~~~~~~~~~~~~~~~~~

THIRD DECADE
Blessedness of weeping

Leader: "Blessed are they who mourn, for they will be comforted."

Meditation

We've all wept. Wept for joy at the birth of a child. Wept in mourning at the death of a loved one. Perhaps we've even wept at others' misfortunes. There is no dearth of occasions for weeping in this world. It seems as though we barely emerge from one deadly disaster only to be plunged back into another, deadlier crisis.

Some might say tears don't challenge injustice. Weeping won't repair war. We can cry and the world turns anyway, spinning as it always has, with us clinging to order and what happiness we can find. True enough. Weeping for the passing of the transient things and people of this world will not restore them. Homes destroyed by flood or fire. Sons and daughters killed in war. Children lost to disease or murder. They will not come back to us simply because we cry for their return. We cry because we must mourn. We must feel the loss and mark it. Give the absence a memorial, a monument.

Christians know the natural world rises from the push and pull of life and death, chaos and structure. We know that what we have and what we are will not always be. We also know the natural world is no product of accident or chance. We live humbly in a vast and complex creation given to us by a loving God. We live *in* this world, but we cannot be *of* it. We can live in his creation because we are his children, intimately bound as creatures of dust to everything he composed from nothing.

But to be *of the world* means we cling to the

things his frail creatures have made, to claim a stake in the world of artifice and invention. When we take up the cross and follow Christ, this world falls away and we can mourn it. And when we do, we are comforted by God's Holy Spirit, because even though we no longer live as men and women of the world, we haven't yet found ourselves among the beauties of heaven.

The blessedness promised isn't that we'll never grieve, but that the Love who created us will be with us always.

(Ten beads, together) Mother Mary... *(page 4)*

Beatitude Promise (TOGETHER) *(page 4)*

FOURTH DECADE

Blessedness of seeking righteousness

Leader: "Blessed are they who hunger and thirst for righteousness, for they will be satisfied."

Meditation

Hungering and thirsting after righteousness is dangerous. The moment we recognize the desire to live in right relationship with God, we place ourselves perilously close to final failure. The chasm between God's righteousness and our independent ability to join ours with his is uncrossable. No amount of work, sacrifice, prayer, or wealth can fill the valley that separates us from the holiness of God.

Why hunger and thirst for what we can't have? Why do we long for love and peace that never comes? From this side of the chasm—our human side—the holiness we desire is unreachable, forever out of our grasp. Nothing we can invent, make, conceive, or discover will propel us into righteousness.

What can we construct from the impermanent world that will itself not be impermanent? Nothing. So why are we so naturally disposed to seek the fulfillment of a purpose, to achieve a goal that cannot by its very nature be satisfied by our works? Our hunger and thirst for righteousness are gifts, graced deficiencies in our souls that drive us to the one who can and will satisfy all our longings.

Architects and engineers could rightly say that this world is designed to be replaced, designed to be old-fashioned and useless when we come to consider our divine end. Light bulbs, car parts, relationships—all serve their proper purpose, but they must be changed out, replaced when they fail.

Once we understand that nothing around us will fill our need for a right relationship with God, we clearly see how obsolete made-things are in satisfying our hunger and thirst. At this instant of clarity, we are blessed. And we are blessed to seek the eternal food and drink of heaven.

(Ten beads, together) Mother Mary… *(page 4)*

Beatitude Promise (TOGETHER) *(page 4)*

FIFTH DECADE

Blessedness of the meek

Leader: "Blessed are the meek, for they will inherit the land."

Meditation

Say the word *meek* out loud several times. To me, *meek* evokes both the image and sound of a mouse—small, squeaky, scurrying around, trying to hide. You probably have someone in your family or among your friends whom you would describe as meek and mild, someone who stands back from the press of the crowd or likes to spend time alone and never gets upset or speaks up with an opinion. The meek and mild are easily bullied, simply swayed.

Meek also makes me think of shyness, introversion, timidity, and passivity. Not at all the type of person who would survive a disaster or wade through a crisis to come out in the end as the heir to the earth. How are the meek blessed?

Why would being passive or timid bring us closer to happiness?

Traditionally, Christian meekness has been thought of as a kind of docility in the face of persecution. Just take the licking and keep on praying for your oppressors. This isn't wrong, just incomplete. Just as there are more ways of doing violence to your soul than outright mortally sinning, there are more ways to be properly meek than adopting a radical pacifism in the face of violence.

One of the most dangerous ways we risk the integrity of our souls is by standing stubbornly against the teachings of Christ and his Church. Having made up our minds about some issue or another, we shut your hearts and minds to further persuasion. No additional information, argument, experience, or authority will alter our stand. We might think this sort of stubbornness is a virtue when it comes to holding to the revelations of Scripture or the truth of dogma.

However, so long as we live we're subject to growing in understanding through instruction and experience. Meekness isn't an order to stand ready to compromise the truth, but rather a way to peace by remaining intellectually and spiritually pliable in the hands of Christ and his Church.

A faithful heart docile enough to be taught anew can let error flow through and out while keeping the clarity of truth intact. A heart stubbornly closed against instruction can only harbor truth and error together in a murky mix that soon festers.

The meek inherit the earth because they allow truth to flush out evil.

(Ten beads, together) Mother Mary… *(page 4)*

Beatitude Promise (TOGETHER) *(page 4)*

SIXTH DECADE
Blessedness of mercy

Leader: "Blessed are the merciful, for they will be shown mercy."

Meditation

When we pray the Our Father, we pray God will forgive our sins in the same way we forgive the sins of others. This is wonderful news if you're inclined to easily forgive those who have sinned against you. But if you're prone to holding grudges or seeking revenge, you might want to meditate on the Our Father and ask yourself whether you want God to treat your sins in the same way you treat others' sins.

Mercy works much the same way. When we show mercy, we are blessed with mercy and we become merciful, filled with mercy. Surely this is a vital element to our happiness here on earth. It is. But why? Think about when you hear the word *mercy* in everyday life. Maybe you've heard it said on a TV crime drama that a convicted criminal is going to throw himself on the mercy of the court. The convict's attorney will plea before the judge for the mildest punishment allowable by law. If the judge is merciful, she will hear the plea, sentence the convict according to law, and then reduce the sentence or suspend it entirely.

For Christians, one element of this everyday use of *mercy* makes sense and another does not. Before mercy can be shown, the criminal must be convicted of a crime and sentenced. Likewise, for a Christian, God's mercy is applied only after justice has been done. In other words, we're first found guilty of our sin, sentenced, and then shown mercy.

For the criminal, mercy is an option. For sinners, mercy is a guarantee. Christ's sacrifice on the cross satisfied divine justice, making us right before the judgment seat. Whatever we owe God for our sins has been paid in full by Christ. We have already been shown mercy. Therefore, showing mercy to those who sin against us is one way we express gratitude to God for his patience with our own sins. Blessedness thrives in mercy because the merciful don't count costs or collect debt, nor do they lend their love or borrow from others. Mercy is freely given and freely received.

(Ten beads, together) Mother Mary… *(page 4)*

Beatitude Promise (TOGETHER) *(page 4)*

SEVENTH DECADE

Blessedness of a pure heart

Leader: "Blessed are the clean of heart, for they will see God."

Meditation

You know the aggravation of having smudges on your glasses or of walking around in a dark house, risking the health of your toes.

Those of us who see can only imagine what it must be like to be blind. But the blind see God just as those who see do. While we are here on this earth, we see him with the eyes of our heart, not the eyes in our head. But if you think this means we know God most intimately through our affections, think again.

In the Christian tradition, the heart is the seat of the soul, the throne upon which the image and likeness of God sits. The heart is the center of our being, the altar for our worship, the tabernacle where the Divine Presence rules. When the heart is restless, worried, distracted, or clogged with sin, our vision of God is obscured, muddled. We find ourselves off-kilter, preoccupied with trivialities, unable to pray, stressed to the breaking point. We must occasionally clean our hearts of smudges, fog, rain, grime, and sin; scrub at the stuck-on spots; and maybe even think about replacing the worn, scratched-up heart for a newer, fresher one.

The Son came to us as a man so we might see with hearts renewed, refreshed, and restored. *Whom* we see is not new. *How* we see him is. Purity of heart is more than good moral behavior and right belief. Behaving well and believing rightly are products of a clear vision of who God is for us. The image and likeness resting in our hearts speaks to the One whose image and likeness they are. If, as the psalms say, deep roars to deep, then we can say that God shows us his Sacred Heart beating in our human hearts. And we see.

(Ten beads, together) Mother Mary… *(page 4)*

Beatitude Promise (TOGETHER) *(page 4)*

EIGHTH DECADE
Blessedness of making peace

Leader: "Blessed are the peacemakers, for they will be called children of God."

Meditation

Most of us know how to make a pot of coffee or a sandwich, or maybe even bread pudding and homemade pasta. But do we know how to make peace?

Shoved hard enough and insulted vigorously enough, most of us could probably be roused to make war. Without much shoving or insult, many of us gladly work to make money. But how many of us will follow an order to make peace?

This beatitude is probably the most hotly contested of the eight Jesus taught. At different times and in different places, it has been used as a justification for absolute pacifism during wartime and nonviolent resistance in civil disobedience.

In his work "On the Sermon on the Mount," Saint Augustine argues that a child of God should be like his Father. This means subjecting the child's tumultuous passions to the rule of reason. When the child's carnal desires are properly tamed, there is peace in his spiritual kingdom, making him more like his Father than before.

Augustine sees this taming process as a matter of allowing superior reason to tame and rule inferior passion. If we understand peace as more than merely the absence of passion or violence, then we must understand peace as something made, brought about. Not an absence, but a real presence. And that real presence is the friendship of Christ among his own people and anyone else who values right reason, putting aside hatred, violence, vengeance, and wrath.

We do know how to make peace so long as we remember how to make friends. If the peaceful heart is the father of a friendship, then the friendship will grow in the peace of the Father.

(Ten beads, together) Mother Mary… *(page 4)*

Beatitude Promise (TOGETHER) *(page 4)*

NINTH DECADE

Blessedness of the persecuted

Leader: "Blessed are they who are persecuted for the sake of righteousness, for theirs is the kingdom of heaven."

Meditation

You've probably seen the t-shirt that reads, "Just Because I'm Paranoid Doesn't Mean They Aren't Out to Get Me!" A joke, of course, but one that portrays the idea that persecution doesn't have to be obvious or even real to be genuinely felt. We've all been snubbed, insulted, humiliated; you may even have been physically attacked or jailed for a real or imagined offense.

Few in the western world have been truly persecuted, violently harassed in the Biblical sense of being persecuted for the faith. Christ promises his disciples that they will follow him on the road to sorrow and death. He doesn't hide or downplay the dangers of preaching the Gospel.

When we stand against the spirit of the world,

that spirit—disobedient, devious, raging mad—pushes back. In western liberal democracies, the worst sorts of persecutions are mitigated by law and custom; we are cushioned against the more deadly forms of opposition to the Gospel because our nations are founded on principles of liberty and reason. Not all Christians are so blessed.

What this means for us is that the persecution of the Church takes on more subtle forms, equally diabolical but not as obviously violent or deadly. In fact, so subtle are some forms of persecution that Christians persecute other Christians, believing all the while that what they do is perfectly moral. Jesus warned that the Gospel would raise the hand of brother against brother and set families at war.

But why are those who are persecuted especially blessed with God's happiness? What's so *happy* about being persecuted? Essential to the perfection of the Christian life is the imitation of Christ on his way to the cross. If we are to *become* Christ, we must *follow* Christ. Not just following his instructions like we would follow a recipe, but following in his footsteps, doing what he did and having done to us what was done to him. Being beaten bloody by the police and executed on false charges are not prerequisites for entering heaven, but being willing and ready to be is.

Pray none of us is given the chance to prove the strength of our hearts. And pray that if the chance comes anyway, we have the fortitude to bear under and follow Christ to our cross.

(Ten beads, together) Mother Mary... *(page 4)*

Beatitude Promise (TOGETHER) *(page 4)*

TENTH DECADE
Blessedness of rejoicing

Leader: "Rejoice and be glad, for your reward will be great in heaven."

Meditation
Many contemporary philosophers and theologians argue that human language and image are woefully inadequate to express or represent the true nature of God.

This isn't a new discovery. Moses knew this when he came upon the burning bush and God told him not to look upon his face because doing so would strike Moses dead. The glory of God is too much, in excess of, over and above anything we can ever comprehend this side of heaven. God tells Moses that his name is "I AM THAT I AM." Not a being like Moses, but Being himself, the pure act of existence.

We can write that sentence. We may even have some limited understanding of what it means. What we can never do is exhaust the divine nature in word or image. God forbade Moses from making graven images of him precisely because all such images would be lies. So, are we left speechless when it comes time to talk about God? How do we express the deepest longings for God except in words and pictures?

We rejoice! If we cannot describe, draw, compose, carve, paint, or build our longings for God, we rejoice. We praise. Without words or images, we praise God for his blessings and his bounty. We can read a psalm or we can sing it. If we sing, we pray twice, Augustine assures us. Words of praise can be written or composed; images of praise can be painted or drawn. But praise itself is the act of purest worship, wholly giving over to the Spirit all we have to give. Praise is jubilation and cheering and crying out and applauding and celebrating.

We Catholics shy away from this sort of emotional display. We are familiar with reverence, dignity, and solemn prayer; but praising God in the way the disciples did at Pentecost makes us profoundly uncomfortable. Can't we just rejoice quietly back here in the last pew? As a matter of fact, we can.

Our deepest delights in God's presence can be expressed in the elation of a heart made pure by grace. Visible expression is well and good, but the clean heart and pure mind can just as readily celebrate in the silence and stillness of a child brought to Christ for his mercy. When we rejoice, we bring ourselves fully to the throne of God. All our words, images, dancing, shouting, clapping—everything comes with us and hears us clearly as his elated children.

(Ten beads, together) Mother Mary... *(page 4)*

Beatitude Promise (TOGETHER) *(page 4)*

Other Titles by Philip Neri Powell, OP

Treasures Old and New

Traditional Prayers for Today's Catholics
ISBN 978-0-7648-1840-0

Treasures Old and New offers a modern approach to traditional prayers. Father Philip Neri Powell, OP, invites you to experience God's presence in praying contemporary novenas and litanies with a traditional and familiar ring.

Treasures Holy and Mystical

A Devotional Journey for Today's Catholics
ISBN 978-0-7648-1913-1

In *Treasures Holy and Mystical,* Father Philip Neri Powell presents devotions for disciples of the twenty-first century. Father Powell's prayers and devotions are rooted in the Catholic tradition, yet they speak to the hearts of today.

For prices and ordering information, call 800-325-9521 or visit us at www.liguori.org.